RADIANT COMPANION

RADIANT COMPANION

POEMS

MATT HART

MONSTER HOUSE PRESS
Bloomington, Indiana

ALSO BY
MATT HART

Who's Who Vivid
Slope Editions

Wolf Face
H_NGM_N BOOKS

Light-Headed
BlazeVOX

Sermons and Lectures Both
Blank and Relentless
Typecast Publishing

Debacle Debacle
H_NGM_N BOOKS

Radiant Action
H_NGM_N BOOKS

PUBLISHED BY MONSTER HOUSE PRESS
BLOOMINGTON, INDIANA

POETRY • MHP-021
SEPTEMBER 2016

FIRST EDITION & PRINTING, SEPTEMBER 2016

COPYRIGHT © 2016
MATT HART

CATALOGING-IN PUBLICATION DATA

HART, MATT (B. 1969)
[POETRY] [UNITED STATES]
RADIANT COMPANION,
MATT HART, PAGES CM—
[FIRST EDITION]

ISBN-10 • 0-9860461-6-7
ISBN-13 • 978-0-9860461-6-2

LIBRARY OF CONGRESS CONTROL NUMBER • 2016911466

COVER DESIGN • RICHARD WEHRENBERG, JR.
INTERIOR DESIGN • ERIC APPLEBY

∞

0 1 2 3 4 5 6 7 8 9

MHP, PO BOX 1548, BLOOMINGTON, IN, 47402

monsterhousepress.com

TABLE OF CONTENTS

*

Catching Light..5
Unsettling the Dust.. 8
This Manic New Trippery..11
Five Red Apples 13
Poem with Some Answers to the Questions 15
Poem with a Chorus by Jawbreaker............................. 18
08/06/14 23
Extraordinary Occasional Romantic.......................... 24
The Friend 27
Reaching the Awe Sound 29
Deafheaven Fried Chicken 32
Dithyrambic Geraniums 35
Matt Hart Running with Daisy, His Dog 36
Radiant Companions...38
Improvised Explosive Invitation Device..................... 40

The Call Up 45

The Locksmith 47

Radiant Reflection... 49

Supermassive Black Squirrel.. 51

Pastoral 53

On Beauty, Etc..54

Some Girls (and Laundry)..56

The Greenhouse...59

Breaking Spring..62

Beauty Will Be Convulsive 64

Deep in Every Wilderness 67

Between Scylla and Charybdis 69

The Panther 71

American Chorus...73

Glitterpuss 75

*

#DearDarkness #DearLight 81

Crowded Valium 86

Redemption Songs 88

Crashaw 92

L Dopa 94

When You Open Your Eyes 95

Lullaby of Ending Things 97

Softer and Softer 99

Nothing Wrong with a Maple 101

Poem for Robert Bly 103

Spring & All 105

Last Poem, Texas 107

Ghost Machine 109

Extraordinary Dinner Party 112

Immediate Neighbors 114

Ode to a Nightingale 118

Acknowledgments, Thanks and a Note

...O most loving soul,
Placed on this earth to love and understand
And from thy presence shed the light of love,
Shall I be mute, ere thou be spoken of?
  —William Wordsworth,
    "The Prelude" (1805)

Could you be the one they talk about?
Hiding inside, behind another door?
Is it only happiness you want?
Does wanting a feeling matter anymore?
  —Hüsker Dü

We are the pulse that beats
and we are the breath that flows
and we will scream along until our hearts stop.
  —The Saddest Landscape

RADIANT COMPANION

CATCHING LIGHT

I love poetry because it makes me love / and presents me life
—Gregory Corso

It's out of my hands, or
    it's all in my hands
        Grace, Faith, Beauty
        O hell
            I'm catching light,
city elm and fir, a loose tinfoil
gum wrapper   This is what there is
Not *all* there is   All there is is so much
more improbable than all the hell
I'll ever catch   The devil
charming everywhere, and
"Dumb green hands," my friend
always writes   Such exclamatory ease
like sitting on this porch, watching
the little rectangle of tinfoil blow past a robin
and the robin never noticing
            only jabbing
                at the earth
I have a problem, which is not believing

people ever really change all that much
Too much muck
        to be enough like weather
        shifting, adjusting, being carried
by the breezes
        Third cup of coffee
            Silver skull on my key ring
reminding me
        of Hamlet, his thinking
too much, then poof, then dust   Philosophy
only matters insofar as it's a poem, free
from the tethers of logic and reason, which are merely
ways of ordering experience, not experience giving
orders—though it does, and its orders will end us—
end *me*—but today I am not a pessimist
I know what "five red apples" means
            in context
I know "noise annoys" yes "dumb green hands"
"little pink birdhouse nailed to a maple"   I know
"thorns of life," "no birds sing," and "This
living hand now warm and capable"
catching the light of the people I love
The devil remains, but so also does the owl,
so also does the frost on its way to this song
Vast distances between us, Scylla and Charybdis,

                I am the demon
                        the demon
                                  the demon,
not evil, just mischievous, in search
      of the miraculous, some new oracle
                          to tell me not to hurt
          so I can tell you not to hurt
      I want our lives to be better, not worse

UNSETTLING THE DUST

—for Katelyn Wolary

As always, with luck, I am just waking up.
The grass outside is sparkling itself.
My life inside is looking at a coffee cup
on the kitchen table that I could almost

touch, if I reached for it, but I won't.
It has a sketch of a typewriter printed on it,
almost a blueprint, almost a ghost. I'm not

sure why I'm telling you that, but perhaps
it's entirely obvious why: I'm setting the scene,
so I can tell you something else, kicking-up dust
in quatrains and tercets. That's just how

it's all shaken out. I try to stay honest
and open with myself. I try to be inclusive
of everybody else. I wonder about the future

and when I will vanish. Then
I do my best to forget about it, refocus
my attention outside my bag body,
the sparkling grass again or some coffee

for the cup. I wonder about butter—if we have any—
I wonder about people, the people I love—
what they're doing while a bee buzzes near me,

for I have stepped outside, and the air swims
with reasons to bite the blossom
off a geranium or the bloom off
an azalea, but instead I bite

the inside of my mouth HARD
chewing wildly on a handful
of unsalted peanuts, which at first I typed

as "unslated" because I'm not really outside,
and it's not really morning. I'm writing with my eye
on something that happened earlier,
but I find it's always such a gift to be present

in language and present in the present
and not to forget. I'm writing to tell you
you have to keep it up—the dailiness

and simplicity, the astonishment and love.
You get to make an owl or an eagle
of yourself. You get to make an image
of the world the way you want it,

not the way it is, not the way
it's always been. Dear Katelyn, a car
just sped by me with hip-hop spilling out of it.

Buckets of raindrops or pigs' ears
or stardust, the voices of people
in summer at a party, counting their blessings:
heartbeat, heartbeat, heartbeat,
thump.

THIS MANIC NEW TRIPPERY

This manic new trippery. Green apples, red meat.
Powdered sugar. O angels. And now, seduced
again by the panic of being and vanishing elegantly

from the squall of this earth. Someday, but not. Some-
day, but not really. My hope is but soon. And here

among the weeds, or out running the thick canopies of trees,
our lungs do their work, most efficiently, mechanically,
in concatenated glee, glowing from the inside

to the outside to the override, crashed on the rocks
and wildly sort of blinking. The crows in rows spray

rags of sound, and I start from where I'm making out
what life has to offer—drinking a beer and/or
reading a book, comprehending nothing. I am

so inside myself. All the EXITs welded shut,
and the angels up above only lounge around smoking

on the cover of a record I remember from forever.
Glistening for no one. We are falling, so we fall. Joy
persists on our kerosened wings. Rebellious

in our ragged jeans, happy being lost. We flail around
stunned, almost singed, fingers crossed.

FIVE RED APPLES

When you give me the slip
marked "five red apples" I am
resigned to it   the number five
the color red   the apples
such nouns   such juice-full
small bombs to throw
against the wall, or wooden fence
to explode   Later, out for a drive
I see a massive eagle take a dive
and a smaller one close behind it
What are they thinking   Three
brown mice   One fat rabbit
I see a HELL sign or a con-
temporary poem
and can't make heads or tails
of it, so crack myself up
wondering why people try to be
so epistemologically certain
what any given sign means
when we all know that
ratiocination deflates us,
and those eagles just float

on the breeze thinking nothing—
or, if not nothing, at least not
"about" things the way we do
And when I get to the store
nobody wonders what "five" means
what "red" means, and the apples
come in so many reflective brightnesses,
awkward shapes and sizes   I pick out
five good ones, firm and unbruised
But then I throw in a fat green one too,
something sort of tart
to make you wonder

POEM WITH SOME ANSWERS TO THE QUESTIONS

—for Nick Demske and Ben Kopel

Sad punk sutra   Sad punk sutra
                              And war
against age, and war
                against the ages
    I curl the blue dumbbell
    I run in the sun
    I tell my students and anyone
                            who will listen
What do you make
        How do you make it
                and Why does it matter
are the only three questions
you ever need to answer
        As a result, my friend leaves word
on his pillow that he will puke
in the face of god with so much
love that god will have no choice
but to tell us all
                      why

in the grand sense, after which
we'll most certainly feel renewed
with purpose or sorry
we ever wanted to know
in the first place,
but at least we'll know
      And the geese overhead
will honk they told us so
or congratulations
depending   What this proves
is that the geese don't speak
unless they have a reason,
and even then what they say
has to be interpreted
by somebody
      Another thing
it proves is that god has a face
to puke in, so the sad punks
should cheer up
and get to work
since puking's one of the things
that punks do best
      I'm 45 and happy,
      not sick about death
Sunset doesn't signal

complete annihilation
just an evolution
toward an ever more pink-
orange consciousness,
then darkness and bewitchment
                          The ghost
of John Keats has lately been seen
beside me when I read poems in public,
and the ghost of Gregory Corso
glows whitely in my fisticuffs
Maybe you can see them now,
riding their heartstrings, gathering
courage   I make poems with words
because I love you, and also because
I believe that you love me
Those are my answers
to the questions

POEM WITH A CHORUS
BY JAWBREAKER

—for Sydney Rains

The word is pain,
and the world is pain,
but the sun on our skin
is enormous and light.

I went out running
this morning, the way
I always do, awkwardly

with lightning. And
at some point I thought
about the song
"Chesterfield King"

by Jawbreaker, which is
a punk rock conversation
poem in the romantic

tradition, if ever one existed
after Coleridge and Wordsworth
made it a thing, then abandoned it.
The chorus goes,

"I took my car and drove it
down the hill by your house—
I drove so fast. The wind

it couldn't cool me down,
so I turned it around
and came back up.
You were waiting

on your steps, steam
showing off your breath
and water in your eyes.

We pulled each other into one,
parkas clinging on the lawn
and kissed right there."
The stanza breaks are mine.

I don't know why
I thought about that
then, or why I'm thinking

about it now, except that
it's a song you should know
if you don't already, and it has
a fragility to it, a vulnerability in its lion-

flaming, punk rock heart that
reminds me of your poems, and how
longing never leaves us as long as

we live, which is lucky,
and even better, I'm suddenly
struck by the image of a rowboat
on the sunset horizon

with one lonely figure
rowing into the distance
out to sea, and in this

image, which is really
the world, I'd like to call out
to the figure in the boat,
to the him or the her,

who is probably you or me or
someone just like us, someone
in need, but they're too far away

to hear me, or I'm too far away
to hear me, and yet,
that doesn't mean I shouldn't
scream and scream

to try and get their attention,
because attention connects us
and generates possibilities, and

possibilities are the stitches
that we use to close
the wounds—the ones
that we inflict, and

the ones inflicted on us.
Yeah, the world is pain,
but attention is rich

and connection changes
everything when we allow it
to sing us, the sun
going down so light

and enormous, the pink
and orange waves,
their marvelous chorus.

I took my car and drove it
down the hill by your house—
I drove so fast. You took
your boat and rowed it out

both to listen and mend.
I'm standing here hoping
to get your attention.

Longing for its own sake
is a letter close to heaven.
Longing and words
continue the world.

08/06/14

I wanted to write a poem,
but I didn't have a poem

Instead I wrote a letter
to a woman named Mary—
not the one you think,
the Mother of God

Then I drank a Vicious IPA

My wife cleaned her car
after months of neglect,
and I painted the mantel
an evergreen color
When I finished, I touched
up the fluff of a pigeon

Coleridge came to tell me
in a vision in a dream

EXTRAORDINARY OCCASIONAL ROMANTIC

—for Calvin Philley

I love the way the children sway,
their lungs the size of tidal waves,
blue solar systems,
giant feedback and dissonance
I wish sometimes I could still be
one of them, but I am no longer
                      one of them
After so much green
light, after all these years
of spirit bloom and hoppy energy,
                    I still keep losing
my voice to the ages   Sometimes
just going to the mailbox,
or out to buy Benadryl
for my white-muzzled
dog, makes me hoarse
Months go by in raindrops
of footnotes   How anxious
and relaxed   I serenade

the deer, half dead in the yard,
                              then stop
only listening to the acorns
crushing hearts   My wife
stirs up potions, as I go
about my business   This one
makes love almost totally
irrelevant, she jokes, but I wonder
if it's funny, and I notice,
not for the first time,
that I'm down on all fours again
in an out-to-pasture gesture
searching for my glasses
or watching a cicada
unzipping its armor,
its eyes tiny strawberries
of ferocious, bad weather
I eat of the grass stain
I lap at the puddles   See
John Clare, his escape
from the asylum   But this is not
England in the early 19th century
This is Ohio in the early 21st
And now that I come to think of it,
most everything is perfect

What else could it be
                            I mean,
I wrote this poem on my phone
while sitting in my car
in a grocery store parking lot
listening to the song
"Chestnut Street"
by Xerxes
08/13/14

THE FRIEND

—for Nate Pritts

The friend lives half in the grass
and half in the chocolate cake,
walks over to your house in the bashful light
of November, or the forceful light of summer.
You put your hand on her shoulder,
or you put your hand on his shoulder.
The friend is indefinite. You are both
so tired, no one ever notices the sleeping bags
inside you and under your eyes when you're talking
together about the glue of this life, the sticky
saturation of bodies into darkness. The friend's crisis
of faith about faith is unnerving in its power
to influence belief, not in or toward some other
higher power, but away from all power in the grass
or the lake with your hand on her shoulder, your hand
on his shoulder. You tell the friend the best things
you can imagine, and every single one of them has
already happened, so you recount them
of great necessity with nostalgic, atomic ferocity,
and one by one by one until many. The eggbirds whistle

the gargantuan trees. The noiserocks fall twisted
into each other's dreams, their colorful paratrooping,
their skinny dark jeans, little black walnuts
to the surface of this earth. You and the friend
remain twisted together, thinking your simultaneous
and inarticulate thoughts in physical lawlessness,
in chemical awkwardness. It is too much
to be so many different things at once. The friend
brings black hole candy to your lips, and jumping
off the rooftops of your city, the experience.
So much confusion—the several layers of exhaustion,
and being a friend with your hands in your pockets,
and the friend's hands in your pockets.
O bitter black walnuts of this parachuted earth!
O gongbirds and appleflocks! The friend
puts her hand on your shoulder. The friend
puts his hand on your shoulder. You find
a higher power when you look.

REACHING THE AWE SOUND

And I'll try to live defeated / Come and see
The Good in everything / Outside animals sound
Come and see / Then lead us all to heaven
    —Protomartyr, "Come and See"

Here and now, this blue winter sky,
                and outside a light
                              frost,
the windows of the houses
            and the windows of the cars
I walk out on the porch, and my glasses
                        fog up
I start my engine to make things warm
Voices swirl around, as a white-muzzled dog
trots by in this marvel of everything good
                        morning
Back inside with the radio on, the word
in the air is terrorist suspects, videos
of child soldiers executing spies   I wrestle
             the juice from an orange
                      in my mouth
I read the beginning of "Song of Myself"

The price of petroleum, a coming election,
a stepped on spear of dead winter grass
                       I do not loafe   I lean
on the counter and call for my daughter
She puts her small self in a puffy blue coat
I put my small self in a black wool sweater
                       I drive her to school
                                   with the radio off
She spells words with the "awe" sound
    in them,
          "awesome,"
                  "outlaw,"
                       "walrus,"
                             "autumn,"
divides by 9's from 108   At the drop-off spot
she gets out of the car   "I love you," I say,
                  "I'll be back to pick you up"
And when she shuts the door, I turn the radio on
Then I turn it back off   At home Greek yogurt
            with pistachios and pecans   a little honey
                I drink life down
                       to a hot cup of coffee
This soft daily-ness, my ordinary "yawp"
                         and "drawer"
                         and "author"

                              and "oft"
This picture of heaven, where there isn't any heaven
              is as good a place as any
                     to begin to make a heaven
          "Either we give ourselves to a course of action,
or we do not give ourselves," wrote
                     William Carlos Williams
The rest of the day, I'm mostly messed up
I go "on my nerve"   "I celebrate myself"
I burn through the world with my hands held out
                         Heaven with the radio off

DEAFHEAVEN FRIED CHICKEN

Grandma's fried chicken was always
the best fried chicken   Even now
my whole face tingles with rosemary
and salt   The first record I ever bought
with my own money that I earned mowing lawns
was KISS *Destroyer*   That's what I called it,

not *Destroyer* by KISS   The first pet I ever had
was a crab that I got in Orlando, Florida
Poor hermit, long white robes, halo afflicted
Indiana   No soul   I went often to church
There was nothing much left
when the dust went to dust

and still does beneath my boots
There's always so much riding on this,
like a bike or a horse down a mountain
blindfolded   Recently, I re-picked-up the guitar
and it was glorious   My singing voice
gargantuan, the Hüsker Dü songs no problem

I put on a sequined jumpsuit and jumped
into the claw   That was also a first,
and I've lived to tell about it   My makeup
was a J.M.W Turner painting   Now it's been
nearly a week, since the surgeon screwed a cityscape
into my jaw, a cityscape that hurts, as all

cityscapes must   I'd love to make a difference,
but Facebook won't cooperate, so this is me
writing whatever I want   Also, my genes
are Deafheaven   "I don't know what you mean
by that," someone says on the street, since Deafheaven's
a band, not a style or a color, not a way down the runway,

but a way to black metal   Well, I think, or maybe I say,
you heard a sound like denim pants but I meant "genes"—
X and Y chromosomes, mitochondria, DNA—some of which is
redundant, I know   Redundancy not a first for me   But
think of a pentagram with a robin's nest in the center   Think
of the delicate and blue several eggs   Now think of me

individually crushing each one of them
and the parents coming back to a terrible scramble
I am distortion and feedback and dregs,
the arsonist holed-up in a fire he is making
Those are my genes, so Deafheaven is an adjective,
at least it is for me   I apply it   Everything

so much longer than it really is or needs to be
Prednisone for breakfast and a second cup of God
The windows unhinged as a schizophrenic snake
I have nothing against it, nor the sun in my blood
I lay the fried chicken on some paper towels to drain
The world reacts violently as always

DITHYRAMBIC GERANIUMS

Because the cranes are craning themselves
Construction giraffes, not the birds'
inky clouds—which are starlings beating
down   The earth full of people—dear
inhuman beings—so covered in war, so tethered
to what fails us   But the starlings go on,
the robins go on, the blackbirds and grackles
and eagles and owls   They go on above
the fraying end games   The massive
machines   The moons and drones and
satellites' sleep   Because because because,
someone thinks   and hears a song
and goes through the whole day
wishing things were different, wishing
the gushing was an actual thing, wishing
for flying, of wax human wings, to hurl
erratic flamebolts of sequins and thunder
Colorful shrapnel   Necessary but stupid
Dithyrambic geraniums always wish
they were birds, but birds, being birds,
don't wish, they get higher

MATT HART RUNNING WITH DAISY, HIS DOG

Big crazy invisible—
Big crazy, and long-tongued

    bright blanket of snow globe

I am one among many brutal footballs
I am one among many spirit calls

        And too many
sounds of pain when the old gray dog
who ain't what she used to be
slips on the ice and goes crash
against the stairs
      again
          Into Satanic diabolical beers
                again
Or rather, that's me,
      imbecilically revisioning
            to feel better
Maybe when it's summer
Maybe next winter

                              Dear washed in the blood
Razor wired in sweaters
                    First down and thirteen
                 What an awfully bad position

And all of life's Goodness seeps
out of our star holes
                              into the next life
                    where nobody moves
because nobody needs to
                    And yet, the old dog runs
           like a rocket at the moon
without any Tramadol
without any Rymadil
An angel's light
body against
my light body,
her body,
old body,
old friend

RADIANT COMPANIONS

—for Jennifer Fortin and Nate Pritts

Nothing's ever ideal
        in this world,
                except what is,
so when we find it
      it becomes urgent
              to hold tight to it,
so as to be calmed and reminded by it
that every second of every day
Truth exists, Beauty exists, Love exists,
and we are better
            for these things—
                    in light
of these things

            Thus, the darknesses
and imperfections we face, even
when they are part of us,
            are woozy and small,
hard black candies we put in our pockets
to savor in daydreams of a righteous new tomorrow

Or, waking up in the morning
with blood red crickets, we go swerving but singing
the ghost of a song, "Runaway" by Bon Jovi,
The Cure's "Just Like Heaven," "I'll Shoot the Moon,"
"(What a) Wonderful World," "All is all is all is all..."
                Life is so full of these little digressions,
unstable longings, unpredictable next minutes
           When two roads *do* converge
in a wood, that's the best thing   Suddenly,
a way forward becomes clear
        through time and space,
the apple trees and birches approving
            powerfully nodding,
                both joyous and strong
"Those who love each other shall be invincible"
              wrote Walt Whitman,
and I am writing this epithalamion forever
    for Nate and Jenny on their way forever
acknowledging how invincible and full of light
    they've become   Two people together
in Beauty, Truth, and Love,
            and all of us are better
for the way it makes a difference,
a brand new constellation
an example to hold *to*

IMPROVISED EXPLOSIVE INVITATION DEVICE

To you with your long faces
long-spun around me, and me
with my long faces long-spun
around me, let us go somewhere soft
to wonder—warm and electrified, forgetting all dread—
our arms wrapped tightly around each other, light

breathing bodies in our light breathing heads
And let us also let this be only the beginning
of a surgical catharsis, a self-indictment
in the jungle, a cataract lifting off into a sky
so blue-eyed-Siberian-husky-blue-eyed
that our awe hangs out exposed to the elements

of awe hanging out exposed to the elements,
which is a good thing, because being exposed is
our natural human predicament and as such
can be used to thwart the habitual
under-amazement and over-concealment
of our bodies' own souls' in floods of numbing

diabolical liquid and too much bird-like anesthetic scree,
the drowsy sounds some babies make to bewitch themselves
when their mothers go deep, complete in complete
darkness, vultures and mavens and preachers and geeks
Let us hurl ourselves out of ourselves into the discomfort
of being anew, aghast, and aglow, limbs screaming   And

treed in our faces, let us ready ourselves, blood stain
and grass stain to bewilder and be wilder, the latter
of course just exactly like the former, except
with its leap-of-faith gap to rabbit-over
into the condor, into the shark, which is back to you
so back to dirt   Now's the time, dear friends, to be

an overheated engine block, irrational radiator,
a reactor so intractable the core melts—not down,
but up—unleashing a beacon surprised
even by itself, smiling like a sea monster
and all the world's devastating money in its mouth
Human heads splitting open   Revelations

Pink blossoms   Asteroids slamming
their crusts into breasts into seas into similitudes
all at once so unnerving that the heart's haywire electric
goes blush with new juice and everything is reoriented

to a gladnesss   O Radiant Companions   Forget
the long faces   Let us roll up our sleeves

and encounter each other for the first time every time,
with all-inclusive kindness, with dear ferocious wonder
There is so much to do   Won't you be
moved   I am singing our souls to you
singing our souls   Can you hear us
in the aftermath
beginning

THE CALL UP

—for Millie Ferguson

Dead or alive, past, present, future
The trees with their balding sudden wigs duly beckon
And business with its greenery, so sick with briefcases
Young fathers and mothers going it alone, tired and alone,
but going it and going it for the good of their own,
which is everybody's good, a generous choice
They too are beckoned   They too are called
Warlords and cops   Teachers and creeps
The angry, ill, and dangerous   The joyous and becalmed
We can always fall asleep, but we can't stay asleep
The crickets in our air bags implore us sing along
And the trees leaning now, as if hammered
in the streets, inebriated streets   calling us
and calling us   O storms of the sun   O radioactive
field mouse   We're running a race against a shadow
with no body, or a body with no shadow, listening at night
as the campfire burns low, its murmur like a fossil
This rollercoaster doesn't stop   not ever   for some of us
Life's not of grace, but of missiles and dashed particles
         Still lives

winging sadly for a better new tomorrow   Go to the
          trees, friends,
and see how they grow, which is   as they can   reaching
as they must   in their nature   which *is* Nature,
their immaculate heads without a single word ever
So much there is to say, which is nothing much to say,
so save your precious breath   unless you can't
when you can't   It's the event, not the structure,
that matters after all, the experience of meanings,
to wonder being called

THE LOCKSMITH

Dear true love,
through the pain in my head,
I'm a dot on the edge
of the evening looking out,
looking over and over
Stupid sky with all its blood
And parking lots on parking lots
as far as the eye can see
They sprawl and spit and yearn
for us   Wheels on the bus
go round and round
All black everything
Sparkling moonlight,
or almost moonlight
It's dusk in Cincinnati now,
and "Angel of Death"
by Slayer wafts up,
meanders across
the cars' expanse expanding
And like a scarecrow
on the horizon,
cut in half

by earth and sky,
a locksmith in his seventies,
working out of his car,
is helping a family
locked out of their car—
a family of immigrants
locked out of their country—
a family of eagles
locked out of the sea
The locksmith is thinking
how foreign they are,
probably illegals,
but he can't be sure
And also he's thinking
rather sadly about moss,
how it becomes us,
or we it, eventually

RADIANT REFLECTION

And commences, some suddenly, some
finally, the musick   The retrograde resplendence
looking   The friends and firebrands   The dear deer
readers   Luminous yard   O   I go to the killing of
    everything
and do it myselfish   Do it hard   And there is nothing
in it to hide behind but lamplight, which is god
if anything ever was, but I don't believe it ever was,

so I am blue in the lost nothing, and crushing
a gnat without ratiocination or other rhinoceros
Over the grass-stain-y hills of   The blood in this body
or your'n   My stomping grounds, they stomp me
Ohio, Indiana, Kentucky   Just roses   noises
The delightful little voices we call to us in revery,
the depths beneath the surfaces of light and winged oranges,

citrus scratched out to mean things   At this juncture
unsurrealistically, I would like to say, Meander and wonder
and wrath   With a sheen on it, an air of something
here or there, pedigreed and vocable   Gray chair
in my living room, shiny metal legs   Gas for the fire

Plants I don't water   Dust   Well   To undress this self
in a feathery of jets is one wish   My people want to know

what's more is   And I can only shake at an angle   This one
or this one   Bluebird or Pterodactyl   Dancing in the kitchen
with pistachios and carrots, lemon coriander vinaigrette
      I regret,
can't remember how to spell, or cast one, and I think this
      goes on
too long in a bewitchcraft of ragged insistence   That,
or, it's never long enough   Always between
Heaven and earth, life is   Beak halves, teeth, coils, claws

When you—if you are who you say you are think you are—
ask if you love, do you wince with marvel at the time it takes
to answer   Affirmative   Effulgence   The sweat
pouring off   Doubly, my heart-cloud is dark at this sentence
Big mouth   Bigger moth   Something struggling to end it,
under hammer   It has come to my attention my intention
is less than   Glorious   Sorrowful mask   I invented
to invention   And wear it all my life

SUPERMASSIVE BLACK SQUIRREL

—for and after Tomaž Šalamun

The beach grass waving brightly at my knees is a sign
The boys on the motorcycle might be
a sign   The brown rabbit and the skunk musk

are not anything, but the oily sheen on my coffee
pretends it's a movie   I should be watching

what it shows me   Two crows attacking each other, or
two men speed-shucking oysters—one of them with purpose,
the other merely glued-to-it, whatever that means

A giant petunia-maker, whatever that means   I say,
lookout, to the former, not the latter, which is a confusion

Crisis manager   Forefinger   Head cheese slathered
on a French baguette   Sign of the cross on a convoy in the
          desert
The fighter pilots cockpit, so the fighter pilots jet   And the
          sound

of a choir breaks open in shards, little blue eggshells,
little tiger-ish roars   And the universe unblossoms

its scurrilous blouse, so to scramble itself with myself and
        yourself
Purple leaves   Reactivity   A violent blue wind
but the spell is incomplete   Wing-smash of centrifuge

Torso-scribbled lemon juice   What's written says,
        Absence, or
Light pours over shadows, like heavy-duty butter cream

And when it's finished, the blank that's left implies a vast
and fuming set of new possibilities   O monster so close
you're inside us already   Hollering at taxis, a little crooked

for our love   Rhinos, weasels, demi-gods, moss
Little girl with bloody nose   Event horizon cluttered
with a billion starry skulls   Winter comes early
when the one who whistles calls

PASTORAL

The squealing of the lamb
comes and goes
against the grass   All day—
Little voices, little dresses
Praying mantis on a bike tire
Rotten board in the floor
Fallen apple   Get to fixing
One event bleeds into another
like an egg yolk into a roadblock:
fried potatoes, piece of toast
White fluff bursts from the brains
of autumn flowers, floats away dizzily,
its fuel, burning dust   And the limbs
of a pear tree reach out to snatch a hawk
from its usual life in the scrambled blue
above   One dog barks and they all start
to bark   Hello, from the scorn and noise-
fat earth   All this, thinks the man
sitting quiet on his porch, sipping
beer from a can, so orange
it almost hurts

ON BEAUTY, ETC.

Rainy walk at noon
                       and cold
to get the blood flowing, to make the blood flow
out among the Westwood dogs, the procrastinating
birds that haven't yet flown   To think about
                       the object,
        "to be recent and strong"
    and my friend in New York
playing two accordions simultaneously
on a stage of air mattresses, singing
herself in Italian collapsing
               "You Are Gorgeous
and I'm Coming"
               With each heavy step
a new spirit within me   an absence as a presence
               no machines,
                   only ghosts
Stay close to experience, I remind myself
        Connect another star   These
spasming white flowers, whatever they are
                      Now
the extremists launch attacks on Kirkuk

Someone laughs hard in an unseen backyard
I breathe in and out to get the recent drugs out,
a surgical procedure, so not of recreation
                        "Everything Ravaged,
                                    Everything Burned,"
a story about Vikings, a story about brutality,
waves of love, harsh reality   In a video
          at the Contemporary Art Center
Mexican construction workers throw bricks
at each other with joy in their hands, with grins
on their faces
                O blood eagle
                              I don't know what
          these things have to do
with aesthetics, but
Beauty and Ugliness reign in the brain
and color the world in a wide brilliant stain   Purple
white and green, as the spit turns to snow
                                The breath
steaming out of my mouth is no angel
                "Richlier burn, ye clouds"

SOME GIRLS (AND LAUNDRY)

The hot pink, purple morning glories
erupted this morning while I was distracted

looking again at the album cover for *Some Girls*
by The Rolling Stones   Have you
seen it   If not, take a second and imagine

a gallery full of Andy Warhol screen prints
eating an advertisement for a 1970s punk rock

beauty parlor, while Judy Garland's version
of "Somewhere Over the Rainbow" and The New York Dolls'
"Personality Crisis" blare simultaneously in the background

and you'll have a pretty good idea what it looks like
Besides the title track (which contains

some of the group's most controversial lyrics)
the album also contains the hits
"Miss You," "Beast of Burden," and "Shattered."

Most critics consider *Some Girls* the Stones'
most punk-sounding record, and I agree, but

critics also note that the album contains elements
of disco and the dirty shuffling blues
the Stones are famous for as well. But the point is

not the record, but rather that I was not
looking very intently at its cover, which was enough

of a distraction to give the flowers—as I said,
morning glories (with their supermassive
open-hearted beauty)—a chance to sneak up

and surprise me, straight from the mouth
of the wolf, as things go. And if that, in and of itself, isn't

wonderful enough, let me tell you
that a little day-glo, green-yellow-black and orange-white
caterpillar has taken up residence on the stem

of one of the flowers. What could be better? Well, again,
let me tell you: The caterpillar's name is Laundry.

Now, I know what you're thinking: Laundry is
a really weird name for a caterpillar, but
the fact is any name's weird for a caterpillar,

and anyway it was my nine-year old daughter,
Agnes, and her eight-year old friend, Grace,

who named it, so I bet it's less weird to you now
than it would be if I had been the one
to name it, but the truth is, if I had been the one

to name it, I would've named it "All Songs
Composed by Mick Jagger and Keith Richards, Copyright

1978, Except as Noted" which you have to admit
is one of the weirdest names ever,
especially for a caterpillar named Laundry

THE GREENHOUSE

—for Sam McCormick

When you open your money,
you are waiting in the white
frozen grass for a sunbeam
to strike your cheek
and make it an apple, and already
you can hear upon the wind
your child's voice
as she fake-sings opera
in the shower all your life
It's only one instant,
but just the same
it's every instant
The weight of the sun
and the dead-heading
continue   Later, you stand
before your friends
a gray pillar of moss,
sometimes still teeming
with electrical charges, little ghosts
of a power that used to be raw   And vital
And dangerous   Of great urgency

to someone   And you recite
words from a book where the end
is always different, depending
on the hour, depending on the listener
You find yourself tired,
your hands up over your head
in surrender to a question
How much money does it take
to get to heaven   The angels
gag on a permanent rag
Molotov cocktails
with porcelain wings
You hammer and claw and make noise
at yourself, and the hammer
keeps banging
until a pine tree falls out—out
of your money and into your mouth—
through glass
basement floorboards
and over the sky,
which is an image
you can live with, live with
or die   The pink comes back
to your cheeks overnight
You've been standing

in the cold for a mighty long time
It's time to find your love
in the greenhouse

BREAKING SPRING

seems like a good way to say
I spent all last week feeling helpless
and talking about it in terms of not being

Why can't compassion change our lives
even half so completely as a suicide bomber,
or half so immediately as a natural disaster

Big ideas get me nowhere, so
the fact that breaking spring feels better
than cracking up is at least a start

toward a walk through Washington Park,
its trees in pink blossom, its white-yellow-purple
Tomorrow I will talk about *Frankenstein*

in bed and then I will talk about it with people
who are sleeping   I will say that it's a book
about artistic responsibility   I will

say it's alive   It's alive   And some number
of eyes will stare back at me without believing
any of it matters, or without believing

it matters for them   And what can I say
to convince them   I have only my love
to recommend it beyond what it already is

My suspect credibility upon the rockets
of birds, the soft parts of people, the oceans'
inevitable, cyclical weeping   Who has time
for poetry has more time than they deserve

BEAUTY WILL BE CONVULSIVE...

It makes no sense,
the ratcheting of skulls
Or it makes only sense,
which is loosely   Blueberries

for breakfast in a bone
white bowl, the back door
flung open to a grassy
broken city   I am at the end

of my hope, singing this note
to somebody faraway who
can't hear me and doesn't
want to   Often, we don't

know whether the things we think,
say, or do arrive on the doorstep
with any real impact, or make
any real difference to the people

they're aimed at   So I just continue
unraveling myself—stupid oak
in a tornado through a living
room window   Last night,

I had a dream about a creature
barely alive—or already dead—
whining and scratching in the chimney,
because of something I watched

on TV before bed, or because
of a call I received from my wife
at work about a baby possum
crawling over my daughter's shoes

near a corrugated shed, overgrown
with fuzzy cattails   It's hard to say
which and not mean to say witch
Memory's a place for hide-and-seek

I'm not unhappy, drinking this
thoughtless clear water from a thermos
I'm more acutely in awe of how
things continue   The world

a gray smudge of cop
cars on the horizon, and yet
there isn't any horizon, there are
only more smudges—a hole

or a bloom or a sculpture of an idiot,
thinking through the distance
of what comes between us,
soft and unreactive in the dust's
empty quiet

DEEP IN EVERY WILDERNESS

there is a lonely, sometimes angry, star
The fires rage for weeks and months,
sometimes years, until the core begins
to collapse on itself, to melt
into the bewilderment
of an angry god, where it becomes
a concentrated spark on the verge
of a war, dangling little mouse,
among eagles, torn apart
                        Everywhere one looks
the deep shadow of a maple,
the storefront windows   The dogs
of evil roam the lake's embankments
where people go to baptize
in a blood orange zest
of porous looking children
         Faux snowmen
                    Mashed potato
pancakes   Inchworms on the walls
When anybody falls into a well
it's horrific—especially when it's an angel
with six inch claws, or a teenager

minding his own dark business
on a corner, even a beat cop
with raspberries pouring out
of his nostrils, the juice, clots of seeds,
which in time only grow into who knows
what horrors   Medusa vs. basilisk
                    Storming the pastoral
            with automatic weapons
        The clouds look as sweet
as bleating sheep, but they're not
They're bewitching, or they're rabbit fluff,
cotton candy dandelion
marshmallow pillow
Darker and darker and darker
we drop   Deep
in every wilderness,
the twitching muscle stops

BETWEEN SCYLLA AND CHARYBDIS

I read Aquinas, doubting everything   Or,
I read Walt Whitman on immortality, feeling puffy
and then walk myself over to an oyster
Beautiful horse gently licking my palm
How I love the way it all makes me Me—
drinking black coffee, imagining eggs, always
forking over whatever I know, including my tongue
American rapture, atomic pajamas

I wanna live forever frugally in bright lights
with long suffering   My family miles away
from me, laughing at the beach, both
with it and at it   Quadrupel ale
with a Lucifer face   And a fire inside it
erupts and consumes the high beams of this body—
mine and yours, which is the same body,

significantly, the more imperfect the union
the more likely words coalesce into a mantra
Mighty Mighty Mighty Mighty Mighty Mighty Mighty
Moe   means nothing not followed by an accent

speaking broadly in multiple languages all at once
My cross still a salt lick to bear, so
my loss   I lay around in bed
not ashamed and not fluffed and not

decoratively ruffled   Actually
it's not even my bed   My heart is not
in it   If you want to know the truth,
we're two weeks on an island, between
a rock and a hard place   The best part's
getting drunk on the aforementioned oysters,
knowing that the sea is everywhere
around us, living and dying, mostly running

in place   Shotgun and sugar
and shortbread and shitty   T-shirt
and whisper, clamshack and certainty
Angel voluptuous, unsilent quahog
Awash in the wash in the wash
in

THE PANTHER

No good poetries to lull me goodbye
Life eats earth meat   I bake an apple pie—
or cherry, peach, tri-berry—then die in my mind
to try my hand at elegance   How to make these better
notes   Tree fluff stuffed into bark-sequined dress
Don't mope your weird heartbeat   Don't mope
your weird head   I draw a duck-rabbit for Agnes
in lieu of a "bunny," which I can't draw, but
which she wants   Regardless   Here's a two-fer,
I tell her   Then   Run 5.2 miles with joy in the sun,
read 52 pages in some book deeply puzzled   Or,
I listen to The Slits, then "Don't Cry" by Guns N' Roses
No, I'm not embarrassed   I am scraped a few moments
by a thorn bush   *Monopoly* on Monday   Tuesday
a prescription   Wednesday thinks a single thing
But Rilke's panther in circles obliterates all of us—
black hole in a cage that if we're lucky we can lean on
I take a nap to reconsider it, and when I wake up
something's actually happened for once   Pentagram,
goat, and a sword on my T-shirt   Coffin of raw cotton
The fridge almost magically re-stocked with beer
These things mean more than saying them says,

and I'd celebrate as such, but it's more fun
without me—you, them, us—the bluebirds and deer
Whose bruising belly's in the grass where we graze it
Who's with me   We're so lucky   How we stand us

AMERICAN CHORUS

—for Blake Lipper

because chorus rhymes with darkness
sort of, and we all need an anthem
surging through the spool of us, me and you
and everyone in unison to star-shot.
We'll return there soon enough,
but today's another Tuesday,
and I almost didn't say that, until I did,
and then the computer filled in
April 19, 2016, 1:23PM, and I'm thinking
about how full of poetry and life and love
your poems are and what that means to me,
which is cavernous, calamitous, and vast
in my experience—which is the only experience
I have to tell you—because chorus rhymes
with darkness, sort of, and we all need
an anthem. This afternoon I'm like a wave
of kids screaming together at a punk
rock show and feeling every little electric
joy and every little pinprick pulse as necessary
soul. I should stop and eat a green apple,

or I should digress a little more,
since I really haven't gotten very far
from where I started, but where I started
is with your poems, where the speaker
is often full of drunk wonder, or full
of drunk stars, or just one more cup
of coffee or a cigarette for the road
and burning with the thought of how lucky it is
the sky is endless we're alive, and the chorus
rhymes with darkness, sort of, because
we all need an anthem we can sing
in the heat and the dust, in the talons
or beak of a pissed-off hawk. I'm borrowing
liberally from all your finest thoughts,
because my finest thoughts
are better when we're together
in galactic, emphatic, empathetic
entanglement, which doesn't rhyme
with chorus or darkness or brotherhood—
not even sort of—but it's no less a song.
Thank you for dreaming and squawking
and daring. And please don't forget
when the music begins, throw your love
in the air, go berserk, sing along.

GLITTERPUSS

Whatever happenstance
This is the real
This is already your listening to angel-less
The grass   Right here right now
The white picket fencing
A black hole colliding
with a boy scout troop
delivering mulch to my driveway
Cypress and Enhanced Platinum, but
that's an entirely different experience, like
When will I die   Every second and always
I will paint-racket the night
with its stars of stupid breath
I will write right and right
the wrongs of my people—
my kind   33 and a 1/3
both to show you that I can
and just to show you
I can rapture, and a forest
comes up out of my amazement by the roots,
the hair   Your hair   Why is it so
suspicious, the people talking

too eloquently about popular culture
The merits of mania
I want words to be matches
or not to be at all, to burn us up from the inside
outlandish, which is a desire   When you get to be
a punk rocker forever, a chair or a missile,
and preach the zombie apocalypse dis-topiary
sequence of events, the way I have,
and the people come up to you with shoes
full of drool, and memos full of clever
sentiments, like on an AC/DC record
only not nearly as good, or not nearly
as recorded as history, the groovy,
you'll know exactly what I mean:
baptism in the blood sac of doing more
than a trapeze artist skimming
the alphabet   The dinosaurs, too, used to be
seraphim, I said or I say or I heard
once somewhere, or they used to
fall asleep on God's knees
and his lap was a dog of napalm
and he owned a long chain reaction
of Goodyear Tire stores
that he used to bind Lucifer
in a burnin' ring of fire,

went down down down
and the flames went higher,
but what's so mystifying about it
is it's also a Johnny Cash song
and my life is Nilla Wafers
and a juicebox   The truth is that
most days I wanna kill
every single person on this planet
so much with all my heart
in an instant, because it feels like
the only way to perpetrate an empathetic entanglement
never-ending and then some
Often I have screamed the stripey anthem steeped in moss
to prove that I believe it, though mostly I choose
to play the chameleon mid-argument
These strings of associations,
and your collected disjunctive resistance
are confetti to my ear   The sophist
in sophisticated's got us slurry in a bog,
a bog we made and continue to make
our astringent red whine out of, our brain-spun cotton
candy, trending right now where we roll
Keep rolling keep rolling keep rolling along,
Hydraulics, mascara, and the Second Amendment's
mis-interpretive dance where everybody's

fired and firing   Nasty, brutish and short
And now, the Leviathan wandering the meadow
of beards, all fours, the pancreatic park with its stilt-legged
bears   My nerves disappear the way
a nerve always does   You just go on it,
throbbing, and eventually it stops,
or it gets so bad you pass out in the street
full of taxi cabs and rain, wet, yellow, black
into paisley covered ducks   Eventually the pain
becomes a new way to love, or the reason
you've always wanted for your hatred to have parents
You are knock-kneed jack-o'-lantern-Toyota-truck-rabbit
This head of living lettuce   Radicchio Pinocchio
What could be the clearer   Who among us
has the experience to smoke bomb
the phoenix and crush the apple orchard
and cough up the amusement that drowns us
in its glamour   Not me   No way   I know it
No way   But not you either   We are scabrous together
O Glitterpuss, I punch the fuck out of your honeybun,
crash my holy lung into a giant white moose   I wish to be
inspired, but there's never any juice   Break a nose
with an orange, and drink whatever runs

#DearDarkness
#DearLight

—for Nick Demske

I'm sorry for saying nothing for days
and instead just reading
over and over the poem
you wrote me in the cloud
and trying to divine from it
whether I have wasted too much my life
or my life too much. I think the answer's yes and no,
like it is for everybody else. Today I'll write
comments to my students
about their final projects
on the GIANT Books we read this semester,
and I'll think some more about what else
I might do with the little time I have left
on this earth. That's not a gag or a pose.
I'm just that sentimental.
I'm just that unsophisticated.
#SamuelTaylorColeridge.
who stared into the Vast
imagining his friend

being hammered by nature
until the friend's knees gave out
from the purpling fucked-up awe of it that was.
"Richlier burn ye clouds,"
Coleridge then spit into the Void
before spitting was even a thing
people did, after which *his* knees gave out
vicariously. What a world it must have been.
#GregoryCorso,
who flattened the whole messed up mess of it
in a spasm of spasm
to make it more the ruin
as he felt it, but somehow
that was a good thing
at the same time that it was total obliteration.
"I love poetry because poetry makes me love
and presents me life," he wrote,
but by most accounts it was complicated,
and he was difficult, but very very real,
a very real human being, the best and the worst,
depending. What a world it still is.
Is it okay to love Poetry
more than poems
and to focus on that love? And when one says
"Poetry," as I just did—out loud to my fireplace

sounding like wind—that is, when I typed the word,
can one mean not poetry, but people—like you,
who embodies so much of what Poetry is to me
and why it matters so much—so much so
that now I just need the people
and not the poems and especially not my own
poems, which fill me with dread
for all the things they aren't
and should be more. Vital. Alive. Full of wonder.
Inspirited wisdom. How'd you get to be
the lord's messenger, Nick, re-teaching us all
about infinite love? And why's the world so sick
I can't stand it? How can I help
when there's all the things
I can't? e.g. Those two little kids, whose bodies
were discovered in a fucking storage bin
in California, and their nine-year old sister
nearly beaten to death and starved,
forced to suffer alone
in a locked car on the street.
My Agnes is nine, Nick.
And she is loved more than anything
ever. But everyone should be. Everyone cherished.
I am not being hyperbolic. I am furious
with sadness. And I know

that with that "news item"
about the murdered and abused children
this poem just took a turn for the worst
that a poem can ever be, but Jesus,
those little kids are just one among
a million everyday atrocities,
and radiant action, which is the "power"
of art and love to save people,
is increasingly for me ever more
in quotation marks, is increasingly ever more
less than, an idiot's pipe dream. #IdiotLikeMe.
My good luck intact. Sometimes
I wanna tear out my mouth—
in #frustration? in #protest?—
and crush it against the darkness
until the juice runs out like
a cherry tree in the apocalypse,
an apocalypse, which has been happening
over and over again continually
for a whole lot of people,
for a very long time, and I can't help
but think I'm contributing to it, because
rather than doing anything real about it,
I'm just trying to keep it from the people
I love with my love. Is that enough?

Is it anything at all?
Does it flow through the world
in the ways that I pray?
Not trickle down and trickle up.
What I want's an ocean
to wash away what's broken
and leave this place better than I found it.

CROWDED VALIUM

—antonymically, associatively after Peter Gizzi

I will not end here,
where an angel with great
feathery arteries flows
like a cheetah down
a veinous gutter
to a concretized birdbath
beginning to dandelion.
What I will do is read
neglect to myself
to neglect myself
and the side effects'
prescriptions uncoagulated.
I click my heels inflamed
with home and love my sorry
neighbor fiercely, first
with a pencil, then
a poached egg. I will do
the worst of all these things.
Every drug is drinked.
Every drink is dragged.

And the muses make
a cassoulet just beyond
the frame where the golf
course grows weedy
and the less fortunate
among us come to eat
on their knees. Scarves
in waves of blue and green.
A butterfly walks on lava, but
nobody sees it, not even the mean
old-timer on the rocks.
Music isn't dawning.
It's a brand new day,
a beginning with holes
and fractures and ruptures.
Now I understand it
so perfectly, the bewitchment.
Speech wafts sweetly
through the kidneys
of an elephant. Warm
and fully soft for the rest
of our days. Here here.
A silver hatchet. Okey-
dokey. To the slaughter.

REDEMPTION SONGS

—for Ryan Khosla

When I realized all my fictions
were merely a Bob Marley song
dressed up in the maelstrom
of a messed-up storm system,
I started to cry again, and I'm not

even kidding. It was late last night, and I was
standing in my kitchen drinking a glass
of tap water. I'd just watched the second episode
of the second season of *Fear the Walking Dead*,
and I won't spoil it for you, but

a little girl turns zombie and kills her mom.
It touched me somehow horribly, but
the emotional levee was obviously primed
for the breaking already. I guess I miss my dog, and also
most of life as it whizzes by me like the bullet

it sometimes is, and I'm not talking
about whiskey. I'm talking about
a green apple, or that version
of "Redemption Song" that
Johnny Cash did with Joe Strummer.

It's awful, but I loved those guys.
I love that song. I'm glad we have
so many versions of the world
to sift through, meanings as events,
and never structures. And I wish

all my enemies would finally just go to hell
and choke on their own vomit at the bottom
of a staircase they've fallen down
fucked-up again, which makes me
super fucked-up again for even thinking

such horrible things. I'm sorry, but not
so arrested I can't wrap my arms
around a Bradford Pear tree
and ask it for forgiveness,
or wrap my arms around

my daughter and ask her
for forgiveness for my not being home
again for days and nights on end,
because I'm working or reading or
too exhausted, too suspicious, too skeptical

to smile out of my hum-drum, dum-dum
sucker of a mind with its siren of misfiring
synapses and nostalgia. These songs of freedom,
overpowered by funk, ring of fire. As usual,
I'm at a loss. The dots don't connect

no matter how I line them up in the sky
of the night and try to make of them an image
of the asshole or angel I'm probably not, and yet
I hope there's still hope for me and everybody
to be over the top. Maybe it's in loving each other,

in spite of our faults. Maybe it's just in continuing
the conversations, replaying the tracks
that never cease to matter. You
should know that I stopped
in the middle of this stanza

and went for a run, and listened
all through it to *Morning Edition*,
and somehow, through the talk
about Boko Haram, Donald Trump
and James Brown, I realized that

it isn't our flaws that make us
unique, it's all the ways we stack up
extraordinary against them, so
I had to cross the finish line to get to
the finish line/this final next stanza, and now back at it

I feel empty and alive, which is something
you said—something you added to me and into
my life, something I cherish with the other things
I cherish, thrashing and burning as we must
with each other, brothers forever,
this holy, redemption-fueled sky.

CRASHAW

—for Thomas Wagster

Dog barking "Acetate,"
                and the washing machine slurring
My words with best wishes
                      Good luck,
finding yourself or anyone else you can
really connect with deeply, since the images
                          images images
are surfaces surfaces surfaces, multiplying themselves
in the infinite
                    Google that shit
                    Your heart's content

                    This afternoon
I'm reading the aftermath, so present tense,
                and feeling ambivalent,
      how I continue,
poetically nevertheless   Protomartyr, METZ,
            and Samuel Taylor Coleridge

And that "Ode to a Mourning Dove" I've been writing,
                Oo-Woo Oo Oo Oo,
    which is an entirely different
                          poem
and for which this poem will serve as a prequel,
assuming I finish it first, but first

                      A jet crashes
           into a mountain on purpose
        Self-proclaimed Islamic State
I get up and walk around to be empty,
    thinking strings of awful things
            Chlorine gas   Beheadings on a beach
So dumb, so brutal, so ruthless, so blissed

                            Blissed?
"What did the *Lamb*, that he should need,
    When the Woolfe sinnes, himselfe to bleed?"
        One of my best students makes napalm
                      as catharsis

L DOPA

> *I got a headache like a pillow*
> —Steve Albini (Big Black)

I've got a toothache like Steve Albini's
headache   Something inside of me
cracked and alone   A single soul train, or
a blade-of-grass graffiti   You think
you've got it bad, well, it's probably
God's fault   5:17PM is no joke   Saturday
One day after three days of terror
in France   *My Power Is Wrong*
is a terrible book I wrote, so you will
never read it, but some of the words
I might hold onto for dear life, maybe
your dear life, but more likely my own
This is my hymnal, I'm sorry to say   Seventeen
murdered and more on the way   A rhyme
seems in such bad taste right there   No doubt
I doubt everything, but death's the new sunset
My tooth won't stop aching   like a pillow

WHEN YOU OPEN YOUR EYES

The weeds mostly pulse, but
some of them hum—and not
a melody familiar, but words
that aren't words   an X-ray's
excavation of bones that aren't bones

Getting better at anything—
whether you can or you can't—
requires wanting to get better,
more than anything else
This is common sense, but
some people don't know it

Stuck green moth in the haze
of no future   Hostages
threatened with the ends
of the earth   You close
your eyes again and watch the skeletons
of loved ones dance with each other,

then collapse into leaves that you can't tell
apart   At the vanishing point

is another vanishing point, but one where
you, too, are so much smaller
than you used to be   When you turn
to look behind you, the vast is a frog,
and the rolling pin blackness
isn't solved, it dissolves

LULLABY OF ENDING THINGS

And stopped   lucking out
No   the Starbucks   doesn't help
We all need assistance with our human
Volkswagon   The mask I often vomit
Too many crows and an off-and-on
kilter horizon, which is pink and black
and gorgeous with horizontal people—
gods, angels, devils—but mostly sleeping-forever
babies in the ocean or the dirt   All hubris
All metal   Iron Maiden   Judas Priest
We the people have burned down the house
But we live in the house, so we die in the house
The house is the body   The body's full of rocks
Howling corncakes   Robert Frost   Volcanic
bleeding owlets   Cicada socks   And the whirring
white sounds   Peaches and storm doors whizzing
through the night   What this points to is unsettlement,
an anxiety that whatever is is already lost   We need
to eat breakfast   We need to eat lunch   And we can,
lucky for us   Stopped lucking out in the grand sense,
        because—

just because—we stopped taking the broken among us in
   our arms
and rocking them quietly   and singing them softly

SOFTER AND SOFTER

The softening grass
and the softening airport

The softening palace
and the softening bullets

The militants' soft blankets
and beards pulled up
around them   The bags
of soft feathers
in Paul's perfect yard

Just leaves, someone says,
not feathers at all   And Paul's
just a neighbor, not discipled
of the Lord   The cold

air bundles all of it
in hooligans' mischief

and a skull spitting sparks
at the hard upper lip

softens the light
around the face of your love

She washes shadows
while you watch the dishes,

realize the warmth
on your softening tongue

NOTHING WRONG WITH A MAPLE

Go fast, white light, go faster out of sight
The Devil *does* know
      how to row my boat ashore   Hallelujah
Orange juice, a swingset, the creaminess of milk fat
    But first let's pull
        the paper's weight
           Let the wind blow—
          O how I love thee
              thy shadowy grace
        And the moon off its hinges,
Henry David Thoreau
      Owlets   Thunder   This
        nervous blinking page
           All the mulch
              I spread around
        in the ultra-black bramble   Let it not
wash away in the very next rain
And let me,
    just the same,
        stand forever in my backyard
           beneath a maple

             looking up—
     there is nothing wrong with a maple looking up—
and gape in the gap of the thoughts strewn around it

       Pleasantly,
with witchcraft, I return to what befalls   The gone white light,
                                       the Devil as he rows
               Hairy Beard-Tongue
                       Butter-and-Eggs
                    Only for a moment,
                           then it leaves me

POEM FOR ROBERT BLY

It's morning again, but the night's still
got a claw on me—it was no big thing,
just some drinking with friends. And now
I stand on the porch with my coffee, not stirring,

as the sun wanders into the sky—or does it
amble? does it blast or blast off?—definitely
the latter. Meanwhile, I've been staring
at an abandoned spiderweb several minutes

before I even register that that's what it is,
the filaments in tatters, and hung up in its center
the long empty armor of a small golden wasp
pointing in the present to the creature it was.

Brittle and uncritical, it waits in the glare
of the balance like a god (until eventually it won't)—
next severe storm, a cacophony of birdsong.
I don't know the birds or their songs, but

the maple is aswarm with them, and a skull
and crossbones flag, faded by weather, flies
from the top of my daughter's old swingset,
convulsing in the breeze, like it's laugh-out-loud

hysterical. The skull face smiles amiably,
the flag's presence like an owl's. Then I notice
my wife removing what's dead in the geraniums.
Nothing I can say will add to any of this—

other than good morning or I love you,
which is all I ever say. Listen, keep looking,
take notes and be true. Stuff myself silly
with the sky's forgiving blue, the grass

that needs mowing, and a book.

SPRING & ALL

The deer stand around in the post-winter cilia
Gray dirt   Yellow moss   And I want it
to mean something to people, but

how can I explain it, this feeling of relaxedness
and dread in the wake   Last night,

I got into an argument with my wife, and still
it lingers in the air of our house, though things,
I guess, are all worked out   An argument

about nothing and no one   Oatmeal, lavender,
a tub of hot water   Hyacinth pokes up

through what's left of the snow   Meanwhile,
Viet Cong skronk   "Bunker Buster"
I'm listening   Those deer up in heaven above

shouldn't be anywhere near me   We
don't live in the country   We live in the trees

called a city, and not only deer, but people
die here too   The neighbors across the street
are elderly   The storm sirens get tested

every first Wednesday   I want this to matter, but
it's only within me   Hermetic spin cycle   Cloying

afternoon   I am apologetic inside myself for miles
into the earth about my failure to entertain you
and about the anger I carry, but I will not say

I'm sorry   I will not say love   I will sit here
by the window, by the fire, by rote   I will
tremble like a thimble, as the green shoots up,
and disappear a little   Then I won't

LAST-POEM, TEXAS

Dozing this afternoon, as I have
the last several. The light blasts in
through the blinds, though they're closed.
The train comes by every half hour or so,
blaring its whistle to let everyone know. And Sarge,
the English Mastiff, one hundred eighty pounds,
sleeps in the hallway outside my room,
snoring bravely, the only sound in the house.
I wonder, could this be the last poem
in which he appears? I nod and stir, then nod
again. And the images well-up in a long flooded line,
a ridiculous parade that I forget almost
immediately, but for flashes, like in Coleridge,
only not as strange as Coleridge. All of them
explicable—explicable to me: Daisies exploding
from the mouth of my wife. Menacing shadows
with impossible questions—who knows knowing,
knows what? The Sex Pistols final concert
at Winterland where I wasn't. The chorus
to "Doctor Love" by KISS, which Gene Simmons,
allegedly wrote in a Holiday Inn in Evansville,
Indiana in the seventies, when I was a child

in Evansville, Indiana in the seventies.
What a strange little kid. I think I was mostly afraid
from all the screaming. I had nightmares and cared
about other people's feelings. I wanted to be
the peacemaker until I was a teenager,
then I was angry for a chunk of my life.
Now that I have my own family, there is
no screaming in the house. I'd say we're all pretty
happy. We're lightning and light. Melanie, Agnes, Daisy
and me. But I've been away some months for work.
Soon I'll go back, and it'll take some adjusting.
The dissonance of seeing and living with ghosts.
Outside now, someone's dumping recycling
into a bin, the waterfall crash of glass against plastic.
I'm completely awake. I'm the calm
against panic, the panic against calm.
And so too the mastiff, chewing his fake bone.
I can hear his teeth scrape against it
with pleasure. I love and hate
dreaming. It reminds me of home.

GHOST MACHINE

So much gray of light today, I can't forget language
how to do things with words. But soon I will drive

a blue car a long distance. Even now I am happy
for its blueness and the sky's wishful whiteness

and for the driving, the going forth to stop at home.
Three weeks from yesterday, and back in my maple tree,

back in the throttle of finding Ohio, something glowing
as ever, and Agnes and Melanie exactly as ever, but

changed, and I am absolutely entirely changed, not at all
who I was back in August when I left them, headed off

in the opposite direction a semester, I hope somehow
they will both forgive me, will recognize the brand new

flowermouth of me, warped machine, wild dog and scream.
I eat a Honeycrisp apple with peanut butter for breakfast

and think about how I've forgotten nothing. How I want
everything back to normal. The pine needle gutters,

the occasional tantrum, even Daisy, my dog, coming in
with a robin or a rabbit, which has never actually happened,

but if it did, it would be horrible, and I would miss it. I've missed
even what I can imagine when I'm there, when I'm where

I'm supposed to be, but I've also loved being different here,
so much of my time in a possible world, one where I get

a moment to myself and all the rest with language, to talk
about words and the world with words, to talk about empathy,

love, grace, and faith, the sounds so bright and always
so strange, small things hitting the ground with one wing,

an acorn or a meteor, dumb ramshackle fencing,
and the hearts of things hanging in the common air

between us, all the beers between us, association
and disjunction, narration and the saccharine, generations

of questions, the ones you can answer without any help
from anyone, and certainly that you can answer without any

help from me. I am opening the gate and proceeding
to the exit. I'm taking your ghosts, and I'm leaving

my ghost. I'm leaving my nerve-some and impossible
machines. Send me your machines, or your ghosts

will surely miss them, and my ghosts will miss being
all of us together, the all and nothing body of inexplicable

consciousness, the finest entanglements we have made
and we can make.

EXTRAORDINARY DINNER PARTY

—for Mary Anne and Mike Cowgill

"Billboards unlovely as sensible feelings"
    I'm in the kitchen making dinner with friends
O growling white motorcycle,
        my eyes failing off of it   "Can you see it"

"No I can't"   Magnolia magnolia and dogs
        blended into the hard wood floors
    We are not some dusty old lamp   I keep checking

the love, and it's all shining through us
    Our doom is great, but there's so much more
to life than what's advertised on the Internet
        Radio Flyer tricycle, iridescent peacock

Days at the pool and Red Stockings baseball   Then snow
        to our throats in dear old Ohio   Notice
    I have drifted off, then drifted back again   Your hand

on my hand still a humbling thing   The point I am getting to
    is right this way   I beg you with me stay

We run and run faster   "Sometimes a scream is better
             than a thesis," but sometimes both are

enough for all creation, for better or worse—
             the growling is a pang on the outside,
             not the in
  Let us attend us with resonance, not business

Let us be together on the up up and ever   "Language
       did not arise from some form of ratiocination"
We rake with the leaves   We beer into the sidewalk
             Somebody shows up with lightning always
             screwed-up

And lucky strike, we throw ourselves with faith
       into a perfect depth   Owls into a fireplace
Squirrels into an icy wreck   All the rest is left to chance
             Pink-orange-black when we touch each
             other's faces
                   So much possibility and turbulence

IMMEDIATE NEIGHBORS

—for Sam McCormick

At a final cruising altitude of 36,000 feet,
I'm thinking about the Chapter called "The Pipe"
in *Moby-Dick* and also about my student, Sam,
who memorized it in her fingers by typing it
one hundred and thirty-six times, once for each
of the chapters in the book, plus the epilogue,
and then performed it for the class, swaying
back and forth, ghost-typing the air to remember
the words, so that Ahab's human struggle became her own
human struggle, and all of us in tears as we stood
there with our wonder. Tough and shocking, a fragile
new meaning. But what triggered this memory, I don't know—
flying maybe

                        in the air next to clouds,
or this young woman, about the same age as Sam, sitting
beside me, and who's coincidentally also named
Samantha, but goes by Sammy, not Sam, she tells me.
She's never seen clouds this close before, having never flown
in an airplane before, so she's taking pictures and can't stop

chattering, popping bubble gum, shuffling her notes for
>
chemistry—
she's a chemistry major in Minnesota she tells me,
among other things—and through it all, barely listening
I'm remembering remembering and also some
forgetting.
>
I can't remember
my first time flying, but right now I'm flying, so that's something.
If I could only be sweeter and meaner, more voluminous,
it occurs to me—I could rise and then fall and then rise—
like Ziggy Stardust and the Spiders from Mars—and then,
if I could write down some chemical equations, maybe take
a few of you with me to Paradise found or Negative Capability,
I would love that to pieces the way I love any linguistic
>
associations—
connotation to constellation in a few leaps and bounds.
The problem of the poem is to experience its ending, having
already known so beautifully its beginning, by which I mean
an agony of life and deathery, of music and speech, which
>
is given
for a minute, then taken away. The pipe thrown overboard
and lost at sea. Sam's air-typewriter, her struggle to remember.
And this other Samantha, Sammy, she reminds me, her carrot
juice hair and serious green eyes, taking pictures of a plane
from the window of a plane.

      The last three days
in New Orleans I've been a version of sparrows and radio-
activity, and now on my way home to Cincinnati, the Samantha
beside me radiates light, so radiates being. "People only call me
Sammy when I'm drunk" my student Sam once said to me,
drunk, then nearly got arrested driving home
to write a poem.
      And suddenly I'm vividly aware
of all the secrets sitting near me, rising and falling, maybe
rising against me, and I wanna know every one of them.
And also, I wonder if Sam will be okay with this poem? I mean,
the part about her nearly getting arrested's not really my story
to tell—or is it? She was drunk. I called her Sammy.
It all could've ended horribly, but great fortune that it didn't.
Who's story is it? What difference does it make as long as
no one gets hurt? Sam's totally brilliant and deserves
the world's attention, the world's massive love
wherever she can get it, but she's had a rough time
by anybody's measure. Dear Sam, You have beaten
the odds, so you are winning. Be happy. Don't throw
yourself in the drink of any ocean. Keep swaying
in the breeze, ghost-typing
your songs
     As for the title "Immediate Neighbors," well,
I stole it while sneaking a look at Sammy's Quantum Chemistry

notes. Something having to do with particles and the sharing of electrons, but what do I know? I just read giant books and lift off. Chemistry's a total mystery to me. The mystery in chemistry. Coffee, beer, and ibuprofen. I steal everything the best way I can, I suppose, from all my friends and neighbors, the immediate ones and some distant planets. And with that, we've begun our initial descent.

        Current weather in Cincinnati is clear skies, with gusty winds out of the northwest at 10 mph. We should be getting to the gate just a little ahead of schedule and on the
    ground
in about fifteen minutes. On behalf of both myself and the Samanthas, thanks for flying with us. Flight attendants, prepare the cabin.

ODE TO A NIGHTINGALE

—for Russell Dillon

This morning, a sea of summer-
    green in the sky   I'm up early
to go running five miles
    and think about flight for an essay
        "Poetry's for the Birds"

But first, I do last night's dishes,
    eat a Granny Smith apple, and listen again
        to a voicemail from my friend

Russell, while stretching my blasted
    forty-six year old self, which hurts
from playing dodge ball on the trampoline
    with Agnes   Agnes is nine now,
        and her trouncing me at dodge ball

is an entirely different story (so here I won't
    go into it), but in the voicemail, which is
        part of this one, Russell reads

a quiet poem, leaking Freon and sadness, his voice
    a rough blanket   The time signature on the call
says 5:30AM, which means it was 2:30
    in California, the state from where he was
        calling, and when my alarm went off

it was two hours after that   The birds already
    chirping their muted green sun   I made a cup
        of black coffee   The dog ate

a soap bubble   The flowers all alight with bees
    softly buzzed   If this seems merely
notational, it is and it is not—"like a daisy in a centrifuge,"
    Russell's soaring poem notes   Sometimes it's necessary
        to record a breaking heart, to locate one's self

in a faraway haunt   Here in Ohio, I put on my Asics
    I run myself crazy   Hüsker Dü in my earbuds
        and an eight-minute mile, then the sound of wind

chimes and "Repentless" by Slayer   Obliterated
    wind chimes   Obliterated clouds
When I get home, I'll listen again to Russell's poem
    I'll write him this poem
        "Do I wake or sleep"

ACKNOWLEDGMENTS,
THANKS & A NOTE

Thank you to the editors of the following journals where some of the poems in *RADIANT COMPANION* first appeared, sometimes in radically different versions: *(614), The American Reader, The Baffler, Conduit, Cream City Review, A Dozen Nothing, The Great American Lit Mag, Gulf Coast, H_NGM_N, Kenyon Review online, Map Points, Monster House Press, NOÖ Journal, No Tokens, Oversound, POETRY Magazine, Post Road, The Shallow Ends, Sprung Formal,* and *The William & Mary Review.*

Additionally, "Extraordinary Dinner Party" appeared in *February Poetry: An Anthology.* Thank you also to those editors.

*

This book would also not have been possible without a generous Individual Artist Grant from The Shifting Foundation. Thank you David Breskin and Chelsea Hadley.

I am also unceasingly grateful to:

The mighty Richard Wehrenberg, Jr. and Monster House Press.

Mary Biddinger and Noelle Kocot for the very kind blurbs.

My students, friends and colleagues at the Art Academy of Cincinnati.

The University of Texas at Austin, where I was honored to be a Visiting Professor during the Fall semester of 2012, and where some of the earliest pieces in this book materialized.

The Bread Loaf Writers Conference, always and ever.

Ryan Walsh and everyone at The Vermont Studio Center.

Nate Pritts and Eric Appleby, my brothers.

All my love to Melanie and Agnes Hart, the radiant companions of my life.

*

This book is for the punk rock bands that saved my life and for Dean Young, who saved it again.

A NOTE ON THE TYPE & PAPER

Titles set in QUICKSAND.
Body set in ATHELAS.

Printed on Rolland Enviro Book—
a 100% post-consumer waste, recycled,
permanent paper.